EVEN A WOUNDED LION
WANTS TO ROAR

EVEN A WOUNDED LION
WANTS TO ROAR

Saul Suchil with Kathy Gillispie

TAG Publishing, LLC
2030 S. Milam
Amarillo, TX 79109
www.TAGPublishers.com
Office (806) 373-0114
Fax (806) 373-4004
info@TAGPublishers.com

ISBN: 978-1-934606-50-6

First Edition

Copyright © 2013 Saul Suchil

All rights reserved. No part of this book may be reproduced in any form without prior written permission from the publisher. The opinions and conclusions drawn in this book are solely those of the author.

Quantity discounts are available on bulk orders.
Contact info@TAGPublishers.com for more information.

TABLE OF CONTENTS

Preface 7
Chapter 1 11
Chapter 2 19
Chapter 3 27
Chapter 4 33
Chapter 5 41
Chapter 6 47
Chapter 7 55
Chapter 8 67
Chapter 9 73
Chapter 10 81
Chapter 11 91
Chapter 12 103
Chapter 13 115
Chapter 14 123
Chapter 15 133
Between the Lord and Me 139

PREFACE

In the book, *The Last Lecture*, by Randy Pausch, the first chapter is called "An Injured Lion Still Wants to Roar." When I read that title, I knew that the title was describing me. Through all my trials, injuries, and surgeries, I did not want to be different--I just wanted to be like the rest of my friends, I wanted to be as tough as the rest of the football players, and I wanted to be strong...no matter what.

– **Saul Suchil**

Saul came into the Library at the beginning of his senior year and asked me if I would help him find a book. He was not an avid reader and as far as I knew, that book was the first book he had ever checked out. Every day after that, he would come by and tell me how much he enjoyed the book. One day as we were talking, I dared to ask him to tell me his story. Saul is a wonderful storyteller, and I was mesmerized as the words came forth. "Saul," I said, "you need to write your story down.'

"No, ma'am," he said, "nobody knows my whole story."

About three days later he came back. "Mrs. G, I'll make you a deal. If you will write it down, I will tell you my story."

That is how this book came to be. Saul has an incredible story to tell, and if nothing else, it is our prayer that his story will be an encouragement to others. God's handprints are all over Saul's life. We give Him the glory for this story.

– **Kathy Gillispie**

Thank you to Tag Publishing for their willingness to take a chance on two novices.

> *"Everybody may know your name but not your story—Everybody may know what you have done, But not what you have been through."*
>
> — **Unknown**

CHAPTER 1

CHAPTER 1

Friday night football. Gruver, Texas. The spirit that is in the air is contagious. A north wind chills the air, and my bones hurt. This is my senior year, and here I am on the sideline. I should be on the starting line. I suck—I can't do anything right. But the moment I step on the football field all my problems disappear—reality fades away—and I live my dream. I'm playing football.

The band is playing in the background—the bleachers are full of eager fans. Tonight is Homecoming, and the alumni have come home from far and wide. I did not even notice the queen attendants. In fact, I am so focused on the game that I am totally unaware of their presence, much less how they look.

Due to all the distractions, I was not able to focus on my class work all week. Keeping up my grades was most difficult. The halls were decorated with streamers and action heroes. The homecoming attendants were constantly talking about what they were going to wear to the game. Classrooms were filled with chatter about this being our last homecoming as seniors, and in the back of my mind, all I could think about was the fact that this was my senior homecoming, and I was not going to get to play. The annual staff constantly roamed the halls, taking pictures of our memories. We had the "Burning of the GHS," as well as a night of fun and games. As seniors, we were triumphant in all our endeavors; we even won the hall-decorating contest. Distractions were paramount—the teachers surrendered to the cause. We would concentrate next week.

    On Friday, the day of the pep rally, the fire truck arrived at the football field amid sirens and cheers. All the students in the district filled the bleachers, clapping and cheering to the beat of the fight song. It was a beautiful day, and I was on top. The red and black Gruver Greyhound flags were flying high in the breeze; the grass was lush and green. There is probably no lawn in Gruver, Texas, so revered as the Greyhound football field. It is watered and manicured like no other piece of property in the city of Gruver, which has a mere population of twelve hundred people. Every home game, we would see from our classroom windows our coach, Terry Felderhoff, a tall, red-headed giant of a man, walking the field with a snow shovel. Obviously he was not shoveling snow; he was picking up dog poop so we would not dive into it face-first during a tackle. We reminded him, despite his disgust, that it was the softest grass in town!

After school, we did the traditional drag down Broadway toward Main Street; the Greyhound flags which lined the street on both sides were flying in the cool Fall breeze. Yes, the spirit was in the air, and we were going to win, but still my heart was heavy.

Coach had told us all to go home and rest and eat a high-carbohydrate meal. We were going to need lots of energy on this cold night. As I drove home, I knew this night would hold nothing significant for me. It was just another Friday night, another ballgame—and I would be on the sideline. Loneliness enveloped me.

I stood on the sidelines, screaming words of encouragement to the guys who were about to run onto the field. At least my words could be my contribution to the game. The coaches were swatting the starting players on the butt and slapping their helmets with a solid *thump*. Coach told us, "Our potential is greater than their potential, but they have the ability to make us look foolish and silly if you allow them to." *No, sir. Not tonight.* We were ready for our opponent.

The game was a night to remember. By the end of the first quarter, we grabbed a 21-0 lead. Korbin scored on a quarterback run and then threw two touchdown passes to Carson and Beau. During the second quarter, Victor

The 2012 - 2013 Senior Football Players

scored on a run, which put us ahead 27-0 at halftime. As the halftime buzzer sounded, we started running toward the field house. With my limp, I usually lagged behind the rest of the guys, but I could hear my buddy, Cole, behind me. He had dropped a piece of sheet metal on his foot during ag class, and that accident resulted in a surgery that removed part of his second toe. His struggle with his crutches gave me the encouragement I needed to swallow the pain and keep going, even though my legs were killing me. The team took it really hard when Cole got hurt—we depended on him.

Cole and Saul, Co-recipients of the Greyhound Spirit Award.

I glanced up in the stands to see where my parents were sitting. I found my dad first, my fighting man. I am so proud of him. He is my hero. He was one of thirteen children who grew up going back and forth from Mexico to Odessa, Texas. My dad quit school when he was in the third grade, so everything he accomplished came from sheer determination and a strong work ethic. Some of his brothers had broken the law and were sent back to Mexico. Even with all the struggles, my dad wanted a better education and life for his family. It is not that my dad never did anything wrong because he told me stories of his close encounters with the law. Dad dug ditches from sunup to sundown, and then on the weekends, he would get drunk with the guys. Regardless of his mistakes, he had a huge heart. He would do anything for anyone. When Dad was a young man, he took a trip to Mexico, and one day while he was out with his friends, he saw a beautiful young lady in a black dress. He turned to his friends and said, "One day that lady will be my wife."

I turned to look at my mom. Yes, she had aged over the years—she, too, had quit school in the third grade to work the cotton fields and hoe potatoes. Here she was, sitting in the stands on a cold October night, waiting for her youngest son to play. Her waiting had been in vain. I was planted on the sideline, but her support was not based on my performance. She means everything to me. She and I have been through lots of trials together, and we are close. Her support and love are two things I never questioned. Even when I treated her badly, she loved me with an unconditional love. Yes, we had been through a lifetime of pain together . . .

EVEN A WOUNDED LION WANTS TO ROAR

> *"Life is a dream for the wise,
> a game for the fool,
> a comedy for the rich,
> a tragedy for the poor."*
>
> **– Unknown**

CHAPTER 2

CHAPTER 2

Pain. They say pain is a good thing because it is a warning that something is wrong, and pain can remind you that you are still alive. Pain was not *always* a part of my life, but as long as *I* can remember, pain characterized every day of my existence. I was born in Chihuahua, Mexico, on January 17, 1995, to Saul and Leticia Suchil and an older brother, Marco, and an older sister, Cindy. Unlike most babies, I was sick for a good while after I was born and had to stay in the hospital until I could manage on my own. Infections plagued my body, and illness consumed my early days. Dad worked at the cotton gin, and every morning he would get milk from my mom and bring it on the bus to the hospital on his way to work. People would stare at the man carrying the jar of milk on the bus. Where was he going? What was he doing? Dad would ride the bus back home at night and find his wife in tears, crying because her baby was in the hospital. One day, he came home with a baby in his arms. The same people questioned him…is this your baby? What is wrong with your baby? My mom saw my dad walking down the road to our house with the baby. She ran to him, shedding tears of joy because her baby had come home.

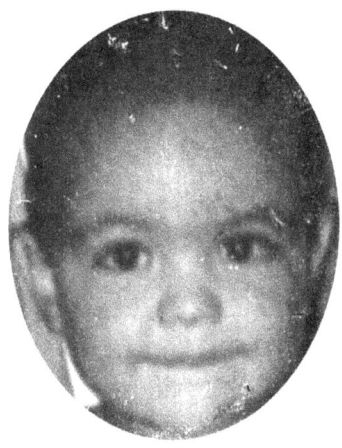

Saul, 18 months

In the days that followed, my parents discovered that I was allergic to milk, and the doctors said I must have a certain type of milk which was very expensive. Dad was thankful for his job, but he did not make much money. So when it came time to pay bills or buy milk for me, he had to make a most difficult decision. Out of desperation, my mom decided she would feed me rice and beans. Somehow, someway, I survived and grew stronger and bigger. For the first time in my early life, I was healthy.

My good health was not to last too long. When I was one year old, I had a very intense ear infection. I would wake up in the mornings with blood and drainage from the infection all over my pillow. The doctor did not know how to cure my illness. My mom left the doctor's office sad and discouraged. Mom had a dear friend that she confided in,

"I don't know what to do. The doctor wants us to go to another town for treatment, and we don't have the money."

Her friend smiled and said, "I know just what you need to do. Kill a rattlesnake, and then skin it. Melt the fat into a liquid and put it into his ears like eardrops." It worked! To this day, I have never had another ear infection.

Apparently, my allergies caused me to be sick most of my young life. Something was wrong with me. I was very sick—I had bronchitis, and my lungs were shutting down. As Mom and I were leaving the doctor's office, an elderly lady in the waiting room asked my mom what was wrong with me.

"His lungs are shutting down—he cannot breathe," my mom said.

"I will tell you what to do," whispered the old lady. "Come home with me, and we will make him well."

We followed her to her house, and there she boiled skunk kidneys for me to eat. I must have been really strong because I survived that meal and lived to tell about it; as a bonus, however, I did recover from the bronchitis.

Saul, Age 3

Both of my parents now had jobs in a bike factory in Chihuahua. They worked separate shifts so at least one parent would be with the children at all times. Finally they were able to make payments on my hospital bills and provide for their little family. One afternoon when I was three years old, Dad came home from working his shift, and Mom left to go to her job at the factory. I asked my dad if I could go outside and play, and he told me no. He was tired—he had been up all night, and he sat down in his favorite chair to watch TV. My patience paid off. Before long, Dad was asleep, and I took off. I got my little truck, and as quietly as a three-year-old can be, I went outside to play. I went out to the road where there was gravel. When I drove my little metal truck across the road, the gravel made a loud noise, which was music to my little ears but made me deaf to the sounds around me. It was that loud noise that changed my life forever. A young lady was driving right into the sun, and she did not see the little three-year-old driving his truck across the road nor did the little three-year-old hear her coming. The car hit me at full speed, and because she did not realize that she had hit me, she dragged my body under the car for several feet. A lady screamed for her to stop. Cindy ran into the house and woke up Dad.

"What?" *You are crazy. Is this a dream?* Dad could not think straight. *He had told Saul not to go outside. How could he have been hit by a car?*

Cindy cried, "Dad, come look out the window. Saul has been run over by a car."

Dad jumped up and looked out of the window in the living room. A circle of people gathered around the tragic accident. Dad ran to where I was and tried to pick me up.

At the hospital, the doctor told my parents my condition was very "iffy." The wheels of the car had run over my legs. And then he let the bomb fall, "He might never walk again."

"God grant me the serenity to accept the things I cannot change; courage to change the things I can; and wisdom to know the difference."

— **Reinhold Niebuhr**

CHAPTER 3

CHAPTER 3

One day can change your life.

One day can ruin your life.

Which day would I choose?

Of course, at the age of three, I was not cognizant enough to make that choice. I am not even sure that my parents told me I might never walk again. I just knew that I was hurt, and I wanted to get well.

The young lady who ran over me told my parents she would pay for my therapy, so through her generosity, I was able to go to therapy once a week. As a three-year-old, I can remember the therapists putting me in water and letting me play with the toys while they worked on me. At home, I would drag myself around the house using my arms to propel me. I am humbled, knowing now the sacrifices my parents made then to ensure that I received good medical care. They would go without many necessities so they would be able to pay my medical bills.

As time passed, I was able to hold onto things and then take a step or two. I would lunge from one piece of furniture to the next, beginning the process of learning to walk all over again. After a year or so, with both hands, I would hold out the bottom of my t-shirt in front of me and hang on for dear life, taking one step after another. My family was so surprised. Neighbors and friends would ask, "How did he learn to walk again? How could this happen?"

Several members of my dad's family lived in the United States. Specifically, I had one uncle who lived in Odessa, so when I was five or six years old, my dad got a visa and moved to Odessa to work so he could send money to our family to pay the bills.

During that time, my health declined, and sickness once again plagued me. I can remember one day in particular when we had just a few beans for our lunch. My brother, sister, and I were asking our mom, "What will we eat tonight?"

I can still see my mom, bowing her head in prayer as she said, "God, please feed my kids. What am I going to do?" Sadness filled our little home.

That afternoon a lady knocked on our door. "I understand that you have some school uniforms that you do not use any more. Would you be willing to sell them to me today?"

Needless to say, Mom sold the uniforms, and with the money she bought food. We ate well that night. Smiles covered our faces because we knew that God loved us and provided for us. Once again our home was a happy place.

That happiness was to last only a while. A blink-of-an-eye moment shattered our elusive happiness. Marco, my older brother, was riding his bicycle down a hill when his sweater caught in the front wheel, throwing him off of the bicycle and causing him to hit the ground with a sudden stop. Not only was he skinned up, but his arms, neck, shoulders, and back were jammed from the fall. Struggling to pay for Marco's injuries as well as my past hospital bill, my parents, once again, were introduced to the all too familiar sacrifices of everyday living. Dad came back to Mexico from Odessa to help Mom take care of our family.

One evening, Dad had gone to the store to pick up a few items that we needed. As he was checking out, he saw the parents of some childhood friends that he had known years ago. He eagerly went over to speak to them and ended up inviting them over to our house to visit. As they shared memories over a meal, Dad told them about our difficulties and the stress brought on by our medical bills. Dad's friend told him that he and his family were living in Gruver, Texas, and that he should come there to find work. "There are several feedlots there, and I'm sure you can find a good job," his friend said. "Come to Gruver with us, and we will help you."

So, with a measure of hope in his heart, Dad left for Gruver, Texas, to find a job. He spoke no English, and hard labor was the extent of his working skills. For him, it was most difficult to find a job. He began by helping the farmers with odd jobs and hauling hay. His childhood friends lived in a house at the feedlot, so with their introductions, Dad was able to mow yards and get enough money to send back to his family. His willingness to work at menial jobs gained him a reputation—Dean Cluck Feed Yard hired him full time as a cowboy and let him stay.

After Dad got his full time job, it was not long before we received word from him that he wanted us to get all our things together and move to Gruver, Texas. I had just completed the second grade. Would this be a move toward more disaster, or would it be a move toward realizing our dreams? For so long, we had lived amidst broken dreams; we couldn't visualize the opportunity that lay before us. All we had to do was take a step of faith.

EVEN A WOUNDED LION WANTS TO ROAR

"When life gives you a hundred reasons to cry, show life that you have a thousand reasons to smile."

— **Unknown**

CHAPTER 4

CHAPTER 4

Change. It is a scary thing. My dad's passion in life was to provide for his family and make life better for us. So, when we came to Gruver, my dad found a job at Dean Cluck Feedyard. There were no houses available for us to rent, In fact, for half of the summer, we lived with friends at the USA Feedyard.

The house we left in Mexico belonged to my parents; they were able to purchase it because they worked at the bike factory which gave them creditability. When we left Mexico to come to Gruver, we asked my mom's friend, the lady who lived a few houses down from us, to watch it and take care of it for us. A few years later we called a neighbor to see how our house was doing, and she said that the lady taking care of our house was carrying stuff out of it every day. My brother went back to Mexico to check on our house. He discovered that the lady had carried our belongings to her house for her own gain. Now our family pictures and childhood possessions were gone.

Finally we progressed from living with friends to finding a house of our own in Gruver. Since Dad was a cowboy at the feedlot, he made around five hundred dollars every two weeks. We were better off than we had ever been before, but paying bills and buying food was difficult. Would our dream of a better life ever come true?

Mom enrolled me in Gruver Elementary, third grade. My teacher was Mrs. Mickey Maupin. Even though she was kind to me, I did not want to be there. I wanted to go home. I could not do what they asked of me, plus, I could not even understand them. They sent me to the Special Education teacher, Mrs. Julie Stedje. Perhaps my first encounters with her are best described in her own words:

I remember Saul's first day of school in Gruver. The third grade teacher he had been assigned to came to find me at lunch. She was carrying a spiral notebook and wearing a look of concern on her face. When asked to write something, Saul had simply drawn a series of shapes and squiggles, starting at the bottom of the page, on the right side. Saul did not know any English. He spoke Spanish, but he did not know how to read or write in Spanish. He did not even know the basic concepts about printing, such as beginning at the top, left-handed side of a page.

Saul was soon assigned to my room for a large part of the school day. The first time he came to my room, he glared at me with a fiercely, defiant look. He sat in a chair, crossed his arms, and refused any attempt at interaction. After several days of the same behavior, I started to get very worried. Saul did not want to get to know me or the other students. He refused to participate in any activity. One morning he was in his regular position, sitting with his arms crossed, glaring at me when one of the other students spotted a very large bug coming across the floor. As we all started to look at the bug, Saul suddenly shouted, "La Cucaracha!" Although I do not speak Spanish, I definitely understood that word – cockroach! I immediately groaned and hurried to the other side of the room. The other students followed my brave example—except for Saul. He quickly captured the roach in a plastic baggie I threw to him. He was our hero! We all gathered around him as he beamed with pride. That infamous cockroach incident proved to be a turning point for Saul. I think he started to feel like a part of our group. He had "saved" us. We had bonded over a bug.

Saul began to very slowly let his guard down. He started to join in as we went over the days of the week, the month of the year, etc. in the mornings. Occasionally we would even get a glimpse of his beautiful smile. Many days were not easy, however. Saul would get upset easily and retreat to his crossed arms defiance. I had to send him to the office one morning because he refused to do anything but glare at me all morning. Obviously Saul wanted to distrust and dislike me. I did not understand this attitude until much later when he could share with me some of his past experiences in school.

Little did Mrs. Stedje know what was behind my defiant attitude. I knew better than to act the way I did toward her. Sometimes I was rude to her. I expected her to let me down, and that was all due to a horrible experience I had in school in Mexico. My second grade teacher was having an affair with the teacher next door. She would leave our class and go next door to see him. One day, we heard them screaming at each other, and she came back to our class visibly upset. Later, I asked her for help, and she slapped me in the face and told me to sit down. From that moment on, I decided that teachers were bad and that they were not to be trusted.

When I enrolled in the third grade at Gruver, I was lucky that I could write my name. Mrs. Stedje reminded me of the struggles we encountered:

We began reading books that were written in English and Spanish. The simple story lines were told in English on one page, then repeated in Spanish on the next. Photographs were included to aid in understanding. Saul loved these books! I know I butchered the Spanish words as I read to him, but I could see him eagerly soak in the familiarity of his native language and the experience of enjoying a book. I began to see Saul's desire to learn. He quickly picked up on many English words in the books. We would laugh at my pronunciation of the Spanish words. He would teach me to say them correctly and encourage me to continue reading to him. Slowly, he began to see that I cared for him and wanted to help him. My many horribly wrong pronunciations of Spanish words showed him that it was okay to try new things and make mistakes. We could laugh as we learned together.

I soon realized why Saul came to Gruver with such a dislike of school and why he was so far behind academically. He was severely dyslexic. Helping Saul learn how to read would be a monumental task. I vividly remember sitting with Saul at our table as he worked to sound out two and three letter words. As he worked to retrieve the sounds of the letters and combine them to form a word, his face would break out in a sweat. One hand would nervously rub his leg while the other hand would draw arching lines under the letters as he worked to make each sound. The harder he worked, the darker the lines would become. By the time he had put the sounds of "i" and "t" together to form the word "it," he might have torn a hole in the paper.

As Saul worked on his reading, I was able to witness a remarkable change in him. His glare of defiance changed to a glimmer of determination. He came in each day ready to do battle. There was never any "a-ha" moment when everything just clicked for him. Each day was pure hard work.

The fact that I knew very little English, coupled with my learning disability, made me really slow. But thanks to Mrs. Stedje, I discovered a desire to do better. I hated doing the homework, but I knew they had worked hard for me. Because they cared, I was willing to try for them.

"I'm not invincible or unstoppable, but I stay strong because it's the only way to survive in this world."

— **Unknown**

CHAPTER 5

CHAPTER 5

I was one of those kids who never stayed home or never sat around watching cartoons on TV. I was always "out there" doing whatever I could to be active. A few months before my third grade school year ended, I just stopped going out. I was content to stay in the house whenever I could. Mom would ask me if I was ok. Now I was always in pain. Mom would say, "Saul, you have just pulled a muscle. It will get better." But the pain did not get better. I was always crying. The pain became intense and unbearable in PE class. I hurt so badly. Now Mom was worried. She took me to Spearman to see Dr. Garnett, and after the examination, he told us that one of my legs was longer than the other leg. He asked for time so he could consult with other doctors. He discovered that my hip socket was dry and the hip bone had come out of the socket. The only reason my leg was attached to my hip was due to skin and muscles holding it together. Dr. Garnett suggested that we go to Dallas to see a doctor at the Scottish Rite Hospital who had more experience in this area of medicine.

When Dad came home from work, we told him what Dr. Garnett said.

"What?" he said. Mom started crying.

"Here we go again," he shouted. I felt horrible. We were still struggling financially and could not speak any English. We were in an ocean without a paddle. My mom prayed and prayed. We had no idea what was going to happen. Dallas was in another world. Where were we going to get the money to make a trip to Dallas, let alone pay the costs of seeing a specialist? But the pain got worse and worse, and soon there was no other choice. I had to go to Dallas to see the doctor there.

Ms. Sylvia Borunda was my interpreter at school. She helped me a lot. Unknown to me at the time, she had talked to all the other teachers at school, and they contributed financially to provide money for my trip to Dallas. My mom never stopped praying. I do not know to this day how it happened, but two plane tickets to Dallas materialized, and we were on our way.

My mom and I were both so afraid. Neither one of us could speak English; we felt like aliens on another planet. We had never flown before and the thought of getting on an airplane terrified us.

Mom and I got on the plane at Amarillo and flew to Dallas. When we got there, we just stood there looking around, scared to death. There were signs everywhere, and we were lost.

Ms. Borunda had made some notes for us, so Mom showed the notes to some people, and we found our way to a taxi outside the airport. The taxi took us to Children's Hospital and let us out. Now what? What was going to happen to us? What was the doctor going to say?

We finally found our way to our doctor, Dr. Birch, and he said, "Well, we need to take x-rays, and then we will 'see.'" What did that mean? He took the x-rays and said, "Come back next month, and we will go over the results and decide what we need to do."

How can we come back? The people helped us so much, but would they do it again?

Mom and I got back on the plane and headed home. We both dreaded telling Dad. How would he handle this news?

When we got home, Dad came in from work. "What did the doctor say?" Mom told him about the x-rays and that we had to go back to Dallas in a month.

"If we need to do it, I'll get you there somehow," Dad said with resolve and grit. "I don't care what I have to do; we will get you back to see the doctor."

We all sat around the table and cried together. I tried not to let it bother me, but it did. The fact that my family would sacrifice everything for me just ate at my insides. Deep inside I knew that they were worried and struggling. I would just try to go on. We had no idea what God was about to do.

EVEN A WOUNDED LION WANTS TO ROAR

*"You never know how strong you
are until being strong
is the only choice you have."*

— **Unknown**

CHAPTER 6

CHAPTER 6

Pride. Secrets. Those are the cloaks we wear so no one will pass judgment on us or smother us with pity. Now there were no cloaks to hide behind. Word spread. Everyone knew about the little boy in school who was going to have surgery on his hip. Every time Dad got paid, we bought less food and saved as much money as we could. The absolute necessities of life were all that Dad allowed us to purchase. There were no frills for the Suchil family.

Mom's fortitude and resilience grew stronger. "This is nothing we have not done before," she would say. "We are a family, and we are going to make it." I remember I would go into the kitchen where she was cooking, and she would tell me, "Saul, stay strong."

The time for my second doctor's appointment came, and we had enough money to purchase the two tickets. Our school counselor let us use her credit card to book the flight, and we gave her the cash we had accumulated. Once again, we packed our bags, having no idea what was ahead for us. This time, the trip to the airport, the flight, and the taxi ride to the hospital were not quite so traumatic for us.

We met with Dr. John Birch, and he pulled the x-ray out of the big envelope and hung it up on the illuminated glass. I had never seen my bones before. He struggled as the dreaded words came out of his mouth, "I have only seen this once. ….the dried bone. …the hip out of the socket. The top few inches of his femur has died. I have no explanation why this happened to him. I think the best option is surgery."

As the interpreter explained in her broken Spanish what the doctor had said, Mom and I both cried. We felt like our world had ended. I was terrified at the thought of surgery. I had never dealt with that word. What was he talking about? As he began to explain to my mom about the surgery, I became terribly afraid. I was trying to understand the doctor's words. I thought to myself, "I have to do something about this. I have to learn English." I would pick out some of the words the doctor was saying, and then I would tell my mom, "This is what I think he is saying."

Dr. Birch cleared his throat and said, "Come back again in a month. I would like to study up on the surgery to make sure we handle this in the best manner."

Come back??? Did he think we lived next door?

We returned home, and once again, we told Dad the

dreaded news. Dad tried to be strong and encourage me. I knew what he was really thinking. I knew it would be hard for him. Instantly, the bitterness which had been seething on the inside suddenly exploded, *"Why me? What did I do? I haven't done anything—we've struggled enough."*

Mom never faltered. "God won't give you something you can't handle—be strong—you will make it." The whole scenario just made me go cold. Even at the age of nine, watching my parents struggle crushed whatever childhood I had left. I wanted to run and play. I wanted to be able to work like everyone else. I began to question myself. To muster any hope at all was just so hard. I just pushed down all my feelings. No feelings at all were better than the ones that kept surfacing.

Watching my mom cry killed me the most. I tried; I really tried to stay strong. It just was not easy. I had no one I could turn to. I knew my parents were there, but they were doing everything they could do to keep a balance in their own lives. My dad was my hero. He meant everything to me.

I was now in the fourth grade, and Mrs. Eva Spivey was my teacher. One day, I was in class in my own little world. Someone tapped me on the shoulder, and it made me mad that someone was bothering me. I looked up, and it was Mrs. Spivey. She smiled at me, and that smile kindled a little spark that told me someone cared.

"What size shoe do you wear?" she asked.

"I think eight," I told her.

A few days later she brought me a gift card so I could buy a new pair of shoes—my mom took me shopping and I bought my first pair of Nike Shocks. They were blue and red. I put them on, and then I took a step. I looked down to see if they were still clean. They were. So I took another step. I checked them again. Mrs. Spivey was always there to support me emotionally. She was always helping me, staying strong by my side. I so appreciated her. However, there was another side that was always raging within me, "Why are you taking things from someone? Don't be weak." That struggle would ruin my day. It was a constant battle for me.

I was determined to be just like everyone else. My determination was short-lived. We would run in PE class, and I would tell the coach that my leg was hurting and that I needed to quit. He would say to me, "Keep running." Then I would tell him that my leg was out of the socket, and he would say, "Keep running." I was so very angry with him, but that anger only served as adrenalin to keep me going.

Mrs. Spivey and Mrs. Stedje continually worked with me, showing a patience that enveloped my very being. Their love and support was like a warm blanket that slowly began to thaw the coldness that so characterized who I was. We argued, we cried, and we laughed together. Because of them, I learned a very important lesson. I learned that I could believe in myself. I learned that I was intelligent and capable of success if I tried hard enough. I also realized that there were a lot of loving people that surrounded me, and those people were committed to help me succeed. My trust in others was still the smallest of mustard seeds.

I had a long way to go.

"You gain strength, courage, and confidence by every experience in which you stop to look fear in the face."

– **Eleanor Roosevelt**

CHAPTER 7

CHAPTER 7

Once again, plagued with struggles and anxiety, we went back to Dallas to talk to Dr. Birch. The interpreter, doing her best, explained his diagnosis. "Whatever surgery we decide to do, it will be an experiment. I will do my best, but I don't know if it will work or not. We will grind down the dead bone, put in a plate, and hope for the best." We set the date for the surgery and went back home.

My world had ended. Everything was bad. Even as a little boy, my frustrations, my anger, and my bitterness were that of an old man. Somehow I kept fighting. My mom continually reminded me to smile. My parents were continually saving money because we had no clue how long we would be in Dallas. Sometimes we did not even buy food in order to save just a few more pennies.

Everyone knew that the surgery had been scheduled, so they gave generously. All of the teachers at school donated to our cause, and because of that, half of me didn't feel alone,

The day Saul left school to go to Dallas

but the other half of me was filled with anger. Even though I tried to hide it, I could feel a boiling inside of me.

I can so remember the surprise going away party they gave for me at school before I left for Dallas. Everyone made good luck cards for me, wishing me a speedy recovery and supporting me the best way they knew how. Mrs. Stedje and Mrs. Spivey were there to wish me well. The kids fought over who would get to push my wheelchair.

For a moment, my little world was filled with fun and games—a party just for me—but after the party, reality stormed in and reminded me that I was different and that I was about to be removed from my friends and my family for a time.

The next day, a friend of our family, Gracie Germany, took off from her job at school and drove Mom and me to Dallas. Gracie spoke English, so she was of great help to us. We told Dad and the family goodbye, and Mom tried so hard to be strong.

Saul's surprise going-away party

As it turned out, I was to be in the hospital a week before my surgery. Gracie got a room in a motel and wished me luck as she walked out the door. There I was in the hospital room, alone with Mom. I felt like life had beaten me. "Okay, you win. I'm done."

Gradually, I learned enough English to communicate with my doctor. He would come by and check on me and talk about the surgery. He told me that if the surgery did not go well, I would be in a cast from my neck down. Then he said, "I have this experiment—I just don't know—you will have to stay here for a long period of time."

Saul and other patients with hospital volunteers

As time passed, I began to notice the other children on my floor. After doubting and complaining to God, my attitude began to change. I was thankful that I could walk. As I watched the other children, I shamed myself. So many of them had stubs for arms and legs. They had come from all over the world—countries like India and Turkey. The little girl from India had to wear a halo on her head with screws attaching it to her skull. Others were in wheelchairs and on crutches. I began to pray and thank God that I could walk, regardless of my severe limp.

I began to communicate with Dr. Birch, and we were able to build a relationship and get along. He would ask me questions, and for the first time, I was able to give him answers.

On the day before my surgery, Gracie drove my dad, my brother, and my sister to Dallas for my surgery. Every night, Mom slept in the recliner in my room, but really—she did not sleep at all. She was exhausted. The fact that she had to sit up all night made me so angry. I knew she was not resting. The night before my surgery, Dad stayed with me in the room, and Mom got to go to the hotel and rest. The doctor told me, "Do not eat or drink anything."

The next morning, I saw the breakfast cart go by, and I saw the chocolate-covered doughnuts going to all the other children. I was so hungry and so angry. Then the orderlies came into my room, loaded me onto a gurney, and took me downstairs to prep me for surgery. I saw my parents and the doctor standing there. The doctor told my parents, "Say goodbye to your little boy—he may not return the same—and say your prayers. We do not know if something might go wrong." So Mom prayed for me, and then she told me goodbye. Throughout my stay at the hospital, I developed a fear of needles. And now they wanted to put an IV into my arm. I was scared. I was afraid of what they were going to do. And I was really angry that they would do that to me. I was determined to win that battle. I fought them hard. For a little guy, I was pretty strong. They tried to calm me down, but I refused to give in. Finally, my dad held me down, and the nurses placed the IV into my arm. The anger inside me reached a boiling point. I had never known such an invasion of anger. The mask came down on my face—people were holding me down—and I felt like a pinned animal. I was terrified. But then the domineering darkness overwhelmed me, and I was asleep.

Eight hours later, I saw something bright. I felt like I was standing in a white room. And then I heard a voice, "Stay strong, stay strong." I was freezing and shaking. I tried to open my eyes, and I heard a voice say, "You are okay—stay strong." They moved me to a different room. I could not get warm. I was still freezing. My body was shaking all over. And I kept fighting—I did not like it here. I wanted to leave. And then I passed out.

When I woke up, Mom was holding my hand. I saw Dad's face. He looked sad. Hours later, in the middle of the night, I woke up again. There were machines all around me and all over me. I slept a lot that first twenty-four hours in a drugged sleep. The next time I woke up, my brother and sister were standing by my bed.

The next day, the doctor came in and told me that everything had gone as he had planned. He had put a plate in my hip and told me not to move my hips at all. After he left, I was mad. I was thirsty, and no one would give me a drink. Why? Where was Mom? She came in my room with wet paper towels and touched my lips. I thought water was the most wonderful thing ever. Even though I was starved, they refused to give me food. It would have made me sick. Dad left that day and took Marco and Cindy home with him. He had to go to work in order to keep the money coming in.

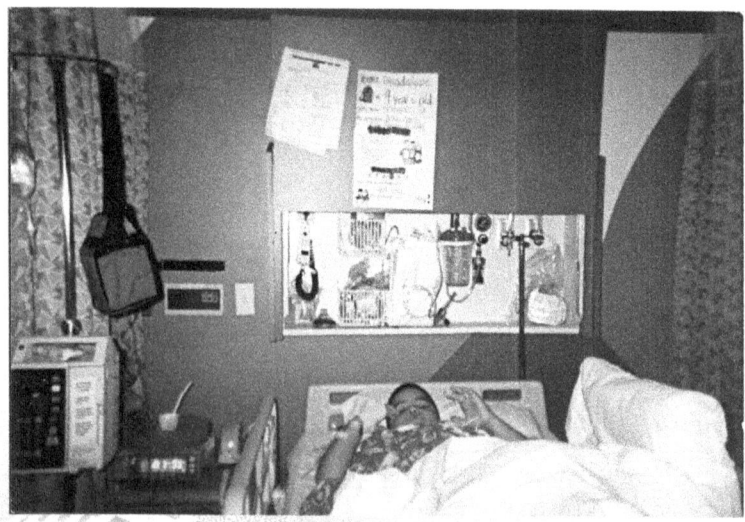

Saul in his hospital bed at Scottish Rite Hospital

Gradually, I was able to drink Gatorade—little sips at a time. Every so often, they would give me another epidural and more morphine for the pain. The nurse would come in and move the pillows and try to arrange me so I would be more comfortable. Mom would grab hold of my leg and move it for the nurse. The pain was unbearable. I would scream at Mom and take my anger and pain out on her. I just knew she was not doing it right. I was so hard on her. I had to stay in bed for a week, confined to the position the nurse desired, and Mom continued to spend hours in the recliner. The nurse would bring the menu by and tell me to circle the things I wanted to eat. Mom and I had no idea what the menu said, so I would just circle "something." Then the food would come for lunch, and I would say, "What is this? I do not like this food."

After that first week, the doctor said I could get out of bed and begin therapy. My failures exasperated me, and once again, anger and frustration consumed my entire being. I would take it out on Mom, and yell unmercifully at her. Yet she was always there, holding my hand, encouraging me. I continued the therapy for a week, and then the doctor surprised us with the announcement that we were ready to go home. Home? Now how were we going to get home? I was in a wheelchair and on crutches. I still could not move my hip—my leg had to be straight out all the time. Mom could not put me on a plane. Dad had just spent all the money he could afford to come to Dallas for my surgery. How were we supposed to pay for another trip from Dallas to Gruver? How were we going to meet those expenses on top of everything else? My dad went to his boss, Monte Cluck, and asked him if he could borrow $1,000.00 to help us get through this. He promised to pay Monte back as quickly as the money became available to him. Not really knowing Monte that well, my dad gathered the money as soon as he could and went to pay Monte back. "No, Saul. That money was my gift to you to help you through this time." My dad could not believe his ears nor could he believe the generosity of this kind man.

"It's hard to forget pain, but it's even harder to remember sweetness. We have no scar to show for happiness. We learn so little from peace."

– Chuck Palahniuk

CHAPTER 8

CHAPTER 8

The ugliness in my life turned me inside out. There was a certain satisfaction in the bitterness that consumed me. The big mistake, however, was that I directed my anger, not at my problems, but at the people who surrounded me.

When the doctor told us we could go home, I heard my parents discussing how they were unable to pay for another trip home. I thought, "Just one more thing to bring them heartache, and it is all because of me." Seeing their hurt and frustration only served to amplify my anger.

And just when I thought there were no more answers, God intervened and used the most precious angel ever to meet our needs. Mrs. Kathy Lindsey was our school nurse, and she and Mrs. Sylvia Borunda, our migrant program director, volunteered to bring a big van and take us home. We saw them get out of the elevator, and in our broken English, we tried to thank them for coming to get us. The trip home was excruciating, and it seemed to take forever to get back to Gruver. But when we got home, I was so thankful to be back. Home had never looked so good to me. People came to visit me to see how I was doing. They showed that they really cared, and I found myself filled with gratitude for the people who stood beside me.

One night at 4:00 a.m., I woke up, startled. I shared a bedroom with Marco, and at first, I thought he had awakened me. Then I realized that I had turned over in the bed—all by myself! I was so excited. It was not a dream. I awakened Marco and told him what had happened. He grunted, "Good."

The longer I missed school, the angrier I became. I would ask God, "Why me? Why did this have to happen to me?" I would watch my parents and family struggle and do without, and then I would get mad again. Every day was the same. I even got to the point where I pushed all my emotions down inside of me. I was determined to get better. I would push myself. I was supposed to be on crutches for what seemed an eternity with no weight on my leg. I was determined to beat the time frame they set for me. Fear consumed me, so I would try to move my leg around by myself.

Mom…Mom…Mom. I was so awful to her. I would treat her badly, and then I would feel really terrible. She had to help me do everything. I could not even go to the bathroom by myself. I got so tired of depending on someone else for everything I did. I was supposed to be a little nine year old boy, running around outside, playing with all my friends. I still harbored lots of anger, mostly at God, because He was allowing me to go through all of these struggles. Mom would look at me and remind me that God would not give me more than I could handle. *Oh, yeah?* When I got in the shower, I was so afraid of falling. Mom would hold out her hand to steady me. She was always there—always encouraging me. No matter what--no matter how I acted—no matter my attitude, Mom never turned away.

That summer I spent most of my days learning to walk and trying to ride my bicycle. It was a summer of physical rehabilitation surrounded by a bitter attitude. My patience was thin, and I did not handle failure well at all. I hated the baby steps I had to take to recover the skills I once knew how to do so easily. *I already learned this—why do I have to start over?* I just wanted to jump back to where I was before my surgery.

Every day Mr. Teal, our Superintendent, would come pick me up in a car because I couldn't get on the bus. For every day that I was on crutches, I began to shut down. Even as a young child, I tried to pray, but discouragement plagued me. Even though I could now take a few steps, everything I did was with anger. I tried to encourage myself, but darkness consumed me. I watched my parents as they continually struggled. We still had to visit the doctor in Dallas, and I could see how my dad was struggling with all of the decisions he had to make. He would pay the bills, and then save the rest of his work check to pay for my doctor bills. Regrettably, I spent those days not caring about anything or anyone. I did not want to depend on other people to help me. I did not want people to feel sorry for me. I just wanted to be healthy and do things on my own. I was determined not to need anything from anyone. I surrounded myself with me, me, me. What a terrible place to be.

EVEN A WOUNDED LION WANTS TO ROAR

"Reality continues to ruin my life."

– **Bill Watterson**

CHAPTER 9

CHAPTER 9

For the most part, miracles do not happen overnight. Nobody wanted a miracle more than me, but that was not God's plan. As I returned to Fifth Grade, I hated the way the kids referred to me. *Oh, Saul, he's the one who had surgery; he's the one with the limp. Saul, be careful, don't hurt yourself. Saul, you can't lift that, it's too heavy.* I just wanted to be normal. Those references were degrading to me and constantly reminded me that I was different. I hated those references. The one bright spot in my day was the fact that I got to go to Mrs. Stedje's class for one period each day. Everyone in her class had learning disabilities, and I felt safe there. I could take off my armor and be myself.

Because I was not on crutches any more, I was able to move about more than I had in a long time. However, the chill of winter brought a pain that caught me off guard. On those very cold days, the stairs killed my feet, my back, my knees and my hips. Because the top part of my right femur had been ground down, my left leg was now longer than my right leg, and I was saddled with painful arthritis. I could not get away from the pain. The pills did not work, and besides, I was taking so many different pills, I threw up the pain pills. My stomach was so messed up due to all the medicine I was taking. I just had to live with the pain. I struggled. I was angry most of the time. I had pushed all my friends away, deciding that I did not need them. I would survive without them.

My life at that time can best be described as a war zone. I decided that everyone was against me. If I walked into a room full of people, I was afraid. I could not trust anyone. I would look for a quick exit. I had a mode of survival that said, "If I don't deal with people, then they won't deal with me." I would see people smile, but I had nothing to smile about. I determined that smiling was a weakness. I thought the whole world was against me.

By Christmas, there was a crack in the hardened ice of my heart. Addy Duran constantly tried to get me to smile, and I blatantly rejected her overtures. But one unexpected day, she caught me off guard, and the stone wall that I had so purposefully built, broke, and a smile spread across my face. Without warning, she snapped her camera to take of picture of the once-mad-little-boy who never smiled.

EVEN A WOUNDED LION WANTS TO ROAR

Make-A-Wish Foundation's limousine

To this day, I am not sure how the miracle happened, but someone from Gruver contacted the Make-A-Wish Foundation in Amarillo and told them about me. When they came to get me, there stood Mom, Marco and Cindy. They loaded up all of us in a limousine and took us to Amarillo. We went to Best Buy, and there, a lady from Amarillo used her credit card and bought me a flat screen TV with games and surround sound system. I know they chose that as my gift because I could not go outside and play.

However, there is one more thing of which I am very sure—that day a miracle began to grow because I realized that people really did care about me. That year the Gruver Lions Club gave me a bicycle to encourage me to exercise. Others had cared before--my parents, my family, Mrs. Spivey, Mrs.

Stedje, Mrs. Lindsey, Mrs. Borunda, and countless others. I had just been so self-consumed I could not see it due to my own self-pity. I had missed the blessings all around me and let my problems rule my life. Oh, the many good things I missed because I had convinced myself that I was all alone and no one cared for me. What a mistake I had made.

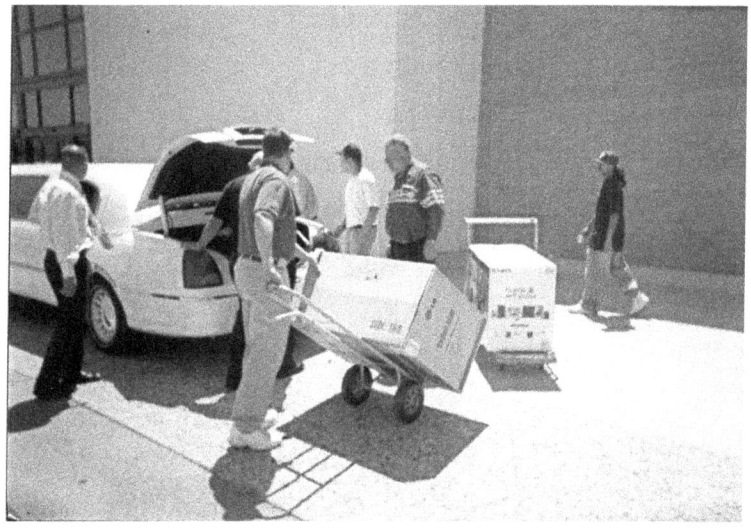

Saul with his big screen TV and surround-sound system

By the sixth grade, I was an independent young man, an army of one. My attitude was so bad that if I were in a crowd, I would look for weaknesses in others, knowing I could use it to hurt them. I was embarrassed to ask for help; I would tell myself, "I CAN DO THIS!" That mindset only made my attitude worse. It turned me cold and bitter toward others.

I guess the thing that hurt me the most was that I could not play football in the sixth grade. I so longed to be a member of the team. The doctor would ask me how I was doing, and I would tell him, "I am fine!" even though my leg hurt so badly. I would tell myself to "go home," but then in the next breath I would say, "No! I am going to do this!"

Since I could not play football, I became the water boy. At least I would be a part of the team. Toward the very end of the season, the coach gave me a suit and let me suit up since I had been released from the doctor. I was part of the team—for real! Yet with any movement at all, my leg throbbed with excruciating pain. I felt like I was weak. And then I would go home. I felt safe there. My mom would tell me how brave I was; that encouragement gave me more motivation to try harder.

As far as school work goes, I struggled. I could not write fast enough to take good notes, so my grades suffered. Coach Davis realized my struggles, so he would give me copies of the notes ahead of class so I could follow him as he taught us science. That helped me tremendously. But the one thing that really caught my attention was the programs that Mrs. Stedje let me watch on the Discovery channel every day. Amazed at the things I saw on that program. I would go to Mrs. Stedje, and we would talk about the program, and she would teach me about the things I had seen on TV. That was the highlight of my day.

Even though anger and bitterness were still very much a part of my life, there were changes taking place that I did not even realize were happening. To this day, I so thank God and trust His timing, because then, at that moment in time, I was ready to receive the miracle that He had for me…even if it were only one baby step at a time.

EVEN A WOUNDED LION WANTS TO ROAR

> "What makes loneliness an anguish is not that I have no one to share my burden, but this: I have only my own burden to bear."
>
> – **Dag Hammarskjold**

CHAPTER 10

CHAPTER 10

What a difference a year can make. My boyhood dreams were now becoming a reality in the seventh grade. I was playing football! Now I was like everyone else! When I put my pads on, all my problems went away. I was in a new and different world. My dreams were coming true. I was ecstatic! For the first time in my life, I felt like I had real friends. These guys were safe to talk to—it was all going to be okay. But by the end of practice, I would be asking myself, "What are you doing? Why are you putting yourself through this?"

I was walking like a mummy. Pain! Pain! Pain consumed me. Mom would offer me painkillers, but I would adamantly refuse, "No! I am fine." Mom would offer to do things for me to make me feel better. I would quickly retort, "No—just leave me alone." But my mom was so faithful to pray for me every night. She would ask God to heal me and to help me. She never lost faith.

A side of me refused to talk to God. Even though I knew He was healing me, I was still angry. I had built up this character that acted like a body cast. It was a safe place to be, and I could fit into it very easily. I was very determined, constantly fighting, never letting down.

Failure was not an option. I was not weak. That self-determined attitude helped me in some ways, but it tore me apart in many other ways. I did not pay attention to other people. I had to be so tough, so I never smiled and definitely was not open to anyone. I had to protect my character. The only thing that made life okay was football.

As a team, we were focused. We were about to be eighth graders, and we were going to be unstoppable! In the halls at school, I was mean. The other kids knew not to mess with me. But one kind young lady, Rachelle, told me I was nothing but a big ol' teddy bear. She saw right through my façade. Truly, it was football that motivated me that year. I kept telling myself, "I can do it." And I would take one more step.

Unknown to me, God put a lady in my life that had a huge impact on me--Mrs. Kimberly Seagler. She was my reading teacher, and at first, I just considered her "another teacher." But she was very nice to me, not easily upset, and very understanding of my mood swings. I was totally surprised that she cared for me like she did. Every time I would test her, she would smile at me. Her smile inspired the little bit of good in me. Then I would leave her classroom, and I would go back to the seedy, bitter side of life.

I started working for Howard and Charlen Stutte the summer of my seventh grade year. Charlen hired me to work on her flowers, clean the barn, work with her horses, and haul hay to the animals. I loved working for them. They were a sweet couple who encouraged me in my daily walk. After football practice, I would go to their house and work on odd jobs. It was a good time for me, and in the following years, I would work for them any time they needed some help. But when I wasn't helping them, I reverted into my shell.

I was living my life according to the music I listened to. Eminem was a white rapper who had a big influence on my attitude. He would rap about not being afraid of anything, about failure not being an option and not backing down. All of these lyrics encouraged rebellion, isolation, and the use of obscene language. Those songs had a horrible influence on me, but I continued to let them be my motivation. Even more than ever, I was an army of one—me, me, me—I don't need you. I got stronger mentally and physically.

I do not know how the teachers put up with me my eighth grade year. My belligerent attitude forever caused problems in the classroom. I was very disruptive and would do anything to irritate my teachers. My "character" grew stronger and stronger—me, me, me. I did not need anyone. However, Mrs. Seagler never gave up on me. We got even closer than before, and I began to realize that I was a happier person when I was in her class. I learned to accept her and trust her with all of my story. I was okay with her knowing my secrets.

In her class, we read the book, *Corner of the Universe*. I really liked that book, and it opened the door for Mrs. Seagler to visit with me about my life and my attitudes. She was the first person that made me aware that I had a good side. When I had time to think, I would think about her and the many things she shared with me. For the first time, I started to like who I was. I liked my good side.

Saul and his parents at his eighth grade graduation

Toward the end of my eighth grade year, a young lady who was a freshman in high school began to talk to me. I did not feel threatened when I talked to her. She told me, "Saul, you have an armor that pushes people away. You are kind, but your heart is locked up." She helped me realize that I wasn't so bad, after all. However, I always guarded my feelings; I was always defensive. I really liked this young lady--we were close.

But like most teenagers, our relationship didn't last too long. I hated myself because I felt so weak. Why did I let myself become so vulnerable? I was "back in the cast of my amour." I could not forget about her. What was wrong with me? Why was I so weak? Basically I just shut down and kept everything on the inside. Bitterness and anger consumed me.

That summer, my two friends and I moved to Channing to work for the Holt's on their ranch. Have you ever been to Channing, Texas? It's a very, very small town, and the house that we were to live in that summer was on the very edge of town. It was eerie to be in that house, so we spent as little time as possible inside. We would go to work at 7:30 a.m. and not come back until 7:00 p.m. We would then eat, go to bed, and then get up at the crack of dawn to build more fence. The land in that area is sand and pasture. It was so hot that summer that while we were building fence, the temperature of the sand burned the rubber off of my boots.

The heat would just leave me without energy. I was too tired to think, but I believe that had a redeeming effect on me. My mind seemed to settle down, and my worries slowly drifted away, but that didn't last for long. More troubles awaited me in the wings.

They say that people are like their dogs. I had a full-blooded Massive Pit Bull. The rage that consumed me could certainly be equated to the rage of a pit bull. His name was Chunky, and he had been my companion for three years. I would take him to the football field, and we would run. After one year of doing this, I could not keep up with him. He was so strong. The summer after my eighth grade year we were inseparable. One nice morning, he wanted me to let him outside. I did as he wished and went about my business messing around outside. I remembered to check on him before I went to two-a-days football practice. He was gone! I looked and looked for him. What had I done? Three hours later, he came back all out of breath and had blood all over him. I was in a hurry to get to football so I just checked him quickly for injuries and then put him in the back yard. I gave him food and water and then scurried off to football practice. After practice, my brother came to the football field to pick me up. He told me that the cops were at our house. Chunky had been found with a goat in his mouth--he had killed 17 goats. The owner told my sister-in-law that the goats cost $75.00 each. I felt really sorry about his dastardly deed. The goats didn't do anything--and Chunky was just having fun. My brother and I paid her for the damages; the owner didn't press charges. She just wanted us to cover the costs of the goats. We took the dog to my brother's place outside of town. Later that month he got out again. I never saw him again.

As if that summer wasn't bad enough, we found out that my mom had diabetes. She was really sick, and that made me feel bad. I couldn't even help her out, and all this time, she had so given everything to care for me. I would pray for her, but my prayers had a bitter ring to them--"God, she didn't do anything to You--she is a good mom. Why did you let this happen to her?"

My parents always lived a good example before me. My dad had always told me that treating people badly was not his thing. And then he would go on to say, "Don't mess with anyone, but don't let others pick on you." I hated bullying, just like my dad hated it. He taught me to be kind, to help others. He fought for what he thought was right--giving sacrificially to help others. He would share with his friends if he had more than they did by saying, "I was there once before. I know how it feels." I wanted to be just like my dad. But it was only a thought. I chose not to act on it.

I suppose my anger and bitterness played with my mind, consuming me. I isolated myself on an island surrounded by waters of loneliness.

> "There's a way of life that looks harmless enough; look again—it leads straight to hell. Sure, those people appear to be having a good time, but all that laughter will end in heartbreak."
>
> – **Proverbs 14:12-13**

The Message

CHAPTER 11

CHAPTER 11

My first day in high school--I was walking down the hall--and there *she* was. I turned my head. I wasn't about to talk to *her*. All the way down the hall, voices swarmed around my head, "You are weak, you are weak. Why do you let her affect you that way?" I was determined, "Tomorrow will be a different day."

I continued to survive by telling myself that I did not care about her, that she wasn't worth my time, and that I was better off without her. But deep inside, I was a lonely, rejected soul. I was just so angry because I let myself care so much for her.

I was to return to the doctor once a year to see how my cartilage was holding out. Because we lived so far away from Dallas, my doctor arranged for me to see a doctor in Lubbock. Having a check up at the beginning of the school year was very important to determine if it would be okay for me to play football. The first visit went great. He took some x-rays and told me that at one point I would need a hip replacement. He looked at me and said, "I can't believe the things you do. The two different lengths of your legs affect your spinal cord, your knees, and your hips." The constant rocking back and forth was causing tremendous wear on my body. And then he said, "I really can't limit you--just take care of yourself, and do what you can do." I was determined I would not be different from the others.

School was well under way, and I loved the fall of the year because it was football season. At least that gave me something to focus on. I convinced myself that I was going to be better than ever. I started going to the weight room, and it was there that I met Tyler. He was in off-season basketball practice, so he wanted to lift because he loved it. I really felt out of place and wondered if I should even be there. Tyler was lifting, and he was three years older than I was. I really looked up to him and admired him. He was kind to me and started talking with me. One night I was doing bench presses, and I dropped the bar on my chest. Tyler helped me get it off my chest, and from then on, he helped me as we continued to lift together. He was my inspiration, and I became even more determined to be like him.

I felt comfortable with Tyler. I tried to keep up with him, but it was impossible. The cycle returned: because I could not keep up with him, I became discouraged and disappointed. I tried to put a smile on my face, but the pain was so intense that I could not smile. "World War III" was tearing me apart. I would go home and say, "Mom, I can't move." And she would say, "Saul, quit complaining." She knew what was going on with me, and she did not like it one bit.

Homecoming activities created a buzz that infected the entire school. All of the guys were talking about getting homecoming dates, and that disgusted me. I was a freshman, and all of the older boys were mobbing our freshmen girls. Besides, who needed a date? Not me, for sure. I was sick of girls.

So who was I kidding? I liked the attention as much as the next guy. There was a young lady who kept smiling at me in the halls. She had long, red hair and beautiful green eyes. I didn't have any classes with her because she was a year older than me. As fate would have it, she left her books in my English class when she went to lunch. So, when I went to English class after lunch, here she came, breezing in, red hair flying, and grabbed up her books. Without even thinking about it, I said, "Ali, why don't you go to Homecoming with me?" The kids were coming into the room now, and several came over to say hello. That ended that! Why had I asked her? I knew she was going to say no. What sophomore girl would go out with a freshman guy--especially me? I kept beating myself up because I had opened my mouth. I thought

I was the disgrace of the whole high school. I wanted to die. What a fool I was to think that I could pull off a date with a pretty girl like Ali.

Embarrassment can turn a person into a heathen. I kept my head down in the halls and refused to speak up in class when the teachers asked questions. I longed to be totally removed from everyone. One day when I was trudging down the hall, I heard a voice call out my name, "Saul.... Saul." I turned around and it was Ali. Oh, no! Here it comes. The ultimate rejection--"I'm sorry, but..." And then she said, "Does the offer still stand?"

"Huh?" I mumbled.

"The offer to go as your date to homecoming..."

"Uh, yeah, sure." I couldn't believe my luck! My life had changed!

On Friday morning, I gave her the traditional homecoming mum, and she wore it proudly all day. The weight of the luxurious mums tugged on the spirited shirts the girls wore for the homecoming game. The shiny bells, hanging from the red and black ribbons, provided just the amount of noise we needed to disrupt our focus in class.

That afternoon, Ali and I agreed to meet at the game so she could enjoy some time with her friends, and I could hang out with the guys. Once we were together, I couldn't say a word. I was so nervous to be on a date with such a beautiful girl. It was the first date for both of us. During halftime, we went to the concession stand and got a drink and a candy bar. More stifled conversation. *Watch the game.* After the game, she asked me if I had a phone number so we could text one another. What was she thinking? Of course I didn't have a phone. So I just hugged her and told her I would see her next week at school. We said our goodbyes, each one going separate directions.

On Sunday afternoon, October 18, 2009, tragedy struck our school and community with a blow that sent us all reeling. Ali and four of her friends were riding around on a Sunday afternoon. She was driving the little red Nissan pickup, and without warning, Ali found herself headed toward the ditch. She jerked and over-corrected, and the pickup rolled. Ali was thrown out of the pickup. She didn't make it. We found out later that she had been texting while driving. How would we ever recover from this senseless tragedy? We were all in a daze for weeks. An eerie quietness filled the hallway. The other girls were out of school due to injuries, and the dark cloud that hovered over our school seemed to take forever to lift.

One evening, I was asleep on the couch at my parents' house. I started to dream of Ali. I startled myself awake, trying to make sense of what had just happened. I talked to Mom to asked her what made me dream like that. Later, I dreamed a second dream. Ali and her mom were beside me. Ali had on a white dress. Her mother saw me looking at her, and said, "Pretty, isn't she?" She gave me a big smile. "Take her home. I'm trusting you. You can kiss her, but that's all. Take her home." When I woke up, tears were cascading down my cheeks. For the first time in a long time, I realized how much I needed God.

In the classroom, things weren't going much better. Because of my disabilities, I could not read as well as my classmates, and that clouded everything. Since I was in the special ed program due to my reading and writing levels, I went to Mrs. Teal's special education class so she could teach me Math Models. My struggles are best described in her words:

When Saul was a freshman in my math class, I was very impressed with his sound reasoning skills. When he came to high school, he was reading several grade levels beneath his peers. His math skills were actually quite strong. What prevented him from reaching his potential were some bad work habits and a lack of confidence. With a little encouragement to slow down and write each step neatly and in an organized manner, he gained confidence in his pre-algebra skills. I thought he was ready to go into the mainstream classroom and take Algebra 1 his sophomore year. When I told him this, he shook his head, and I could tell that, confidence-wise, he wasn't ready.

As his special education teacher, I would keep tabs on his performance in other classes, and I would hear about him "not caring" about his work and being off-task, generally doing anything that would keep from doing work while he was in class. He disliked writing, especially and he struggled to complete his essays and research papers.

There was no way I could go into the regular classroom. I wasn't as smart as my peers, and I sure didn't want to remove any doubts by making a fool of myself in front of them. So, typical of my subversive attitude, I continued in my safe zone, protected by the few I could trust.

The only thing wrong with that mentality is that I could not stay in Mrs. Teal's room all day--I had to go out in the hall between classes. And that is when it happened. I had let my guard down, and when *she* smiled at me, I caved in and started talking to her. I've heard said that your "first love" will hold a place in your heart for the rest of your life. I knew she was dating another guy, but that did not dim my devotion to her. We started hanging out more and more, our conversations deepening in content, covering life issues. I couldn't wait to see her again.

Cesar, one of my dearest friends who was like a member of the family, observed what was going on. "Saul, don't be dumb. You're fallin.'" But I refused to listen to him. When Cesar had moved to Gruver, he had seen a bunch of us playing soccer in the park. One day we asked him to join us. He was eighteen and new in town, and I was in the sixth grade. He started hanging out at our house and became close friends with my older brother. So when my brother started dating, he spent all of his time with his girlfriend, and that left Cesar and me to hang out and watch TV. I noticed that he always watched cartoons--all the time. One day I said to him, "Cesar, you need to get a life."

Saul and his dear friend, Cesar

"Saul, I would give anything if I could be a child again. Life was so much easier then." And then he told me, "Saul, you don't have a childhood. You are way too serious. You need to be a kid. Once your childhood is gone, it's gone."

I told him, "Oh, Cesar, grow up--you are twenty years old and still watching cartoons." I cared about Cesar; he was the first one to ever call me "Gordo." The name stuck--all of my family members still call me "Gordo." I hated myself when I was mean to him. He was my friend, my family, my brother.

I continued to enjoy being around the young lady who was such a bright spot in my life. I would talk to her as often as I could. I knew she was going out with another guy, but that didn't bother me. I was willing to be with her any time I could and for any reason. On Easter weekend, she texted me, "I hate this. We have to end it. This can't happen. I never should have done it. "

What? What was she thinking? I picked up my cell phone and called her. She didn't know what to say to me. So I told her, "I won't accept this until you say it to my face."

"You know I can't," she whined. She never did talk to me face to face.

I hated myself even more. Why had I been so weak to trust her again? Why did I care so much? The bitterness and anger came storming back in.

I called Cesar. He picked me up, and we went crusin'. I told him what had happened. "Hey," I said, "I've got some money. Let's go get some." It didn't take me long to obliterate my troubles. Before I knew it I was gone...long gone. I was drunk out of my mind; the bottom of the bottle was my only friend. That thought kept running through my mind over and over again. Since Cesar was the older one, he was doing all the driving. It didn't take long before we got stopped, and he was arrested. They impounded his truck. I got a MIP (Minor in Possession) ticket. The police put him in jail. They would deal with me later.

A few days later, I received word that I was to dole out 28 hours of community service for my MIP ticket and write a 500 word essay on the effects of alcohol on the human body. I would go to City Hall after athletics and off-season weight lifting, and they would give me my work assignment. Then I would complete my duties around six or seven o'clock and go home and drink some more. I didn't care.

That summer I was worthless. I continued to work at the ranch, but in my spare time, I drank more and more. I did not care who or what I was. I just wanted to get through the day. I didn't even exercise or lift weights. I was at the bottom of the barrel.

What had happened to me? How stupid was I? I had made a fool of myself, I had a MIP ticket, and my dear friend was in jail--all because of me. Whatever made me think that drinking beer would erase my pain and answer my problems? Not only had I brought embarrassment to myself, I had cost my parents more money--again. Was this going to be the way it was for the rest of my life? The "downward spiral" had a strong grip on me.

EVEN A WOUNDED LION WANTS TO ROAR

*"One day can change your life.
One day can ruin you.
That one day is your choice."*

– Unknown

CHAPTER 12

CHAPTER 12

Choices. We make them every day. Sometimes those choices make little to no difference at all, but sometimes, those choices can have a huge impact on our lives. Regardless, choices have outcomes. Definitely I had made some bad choices, and now I was reaping the consequences. How in this world could I turn my life around? I did not like who I was nor did I like who I was becoming.

Some days I didn't care what happened. And then I would go back into my "failure is not an option" mode. I didn't know what I wanted or how I was going to find out.

During our sophomore year, we were reading two different books in English class for Ms. Clark -- *Same Kind of Different as Me* and *The Boy in the Striped Pajamas*. After reading those two books, I discovered that I really liked reading. Those two stories made me realize that other people in life had problems greater than my problems. Gradually my attitude began to change. Mrs. Teal could tell that those stories made a difference:

Saul discovered that he was just like everyone else. His writing skills improved, and when he compared himself to other students in the class, he discovered that others had the same struggles he did. He was very proud when he received his GPA from the counselor. It was an A. He was rather "bummed out" when I had to break it to him that he couldn't be in the National Honor Society because, even though he had an A average, he was on the Minimum Graduation Plan. I think that is when it hit him that his choices in classes were preventing him from reaching his potential. Saul asked if he could be an honor graduate if he got on the Recommended Plan. "You bet!" I said, but because he didn't take Algebra his sophomore year, he would need to take all four mainstream math courses in the next two years--a very difficult, if not impossible, challenge. Saul had some thinking to do.

I thought about what Mrs. Teal had told me. I knew I would like to get out of Special Ed, but I loved being in Mrs. Teal's math class. We could take our time, and I was able to understand what was going on. So one day I mustered enough courage to ask her what I had to do to get out of Special Ed. "You'll have to double up in math," she told me. "You'll have to go to regular classes and there will be less help available to you." I had so many decisions to make--decisions that could possibly break me and leave me totally embarrassed and humiliated. I could be facing a totally new path--one that could totally change my life.

Spring brought the stress that goes with taking the TAKS test. As sophomores, we had to write an essay, and I had no idea if I could pull it off or not. I hated writing. Mrs. Teal would talk with me a lot about different ideas that I could write about. "You can do it," she would tell me. I was so frustrated. I would struggle with writing a half page, and we had to write two pages on the test. Ms. Clark would work with us in class, trying to prepare us for the test ahead. I will never forget the prompt on our test that year: "Write about someone that you look up to." That was so easy for me--I would write about Tyler and the many nights we spent in the weight room and how helped me over and over again. I could tell that my words were flowing. Since the test was untimed, we could stay as long as we needed to finish the test. There were three of us still working, so Mr. Seagler, our principal, and Mrs. Curry, our counselor, brought supper to us. I completed my test at 7:00 p.m. When the test results came back, I had made a 3 out of 4 on my written essay. Ms. Clark and Mrs. Teal were ecstatic. I couldn't believe it!

Later that year, I received word that as a sophomore, I was eligible to apply for the Big Brother Big Sister program. I knew that Mrs. Stedje was in charge of that program, so to be able to work with her again would be special for me. I filled out the application and awaited notification of my interview.

I was glad I was going to be able to see Mrs. Stedje again. Little did I know that she felt the same way:

As I prepared for Saul's interview, I was excited about getting to spend some one-on-one time with him. I was so proud of him for wanting to mentor a younger student. I was filled with pride and amazement as I spent time that day with Saul. He strode into the room a strong, confident, handsome young man. He spoke eloquently about his desire to reach out to an at-risk child since so many others had reached out to him. I silently marveled at his rich vocabulary and his command of the English language. I thanked God for the opportunity to see Saul come full circle - from the hurting child in need of care from others - to the confident young man ready to make a difference in the life of another.

I felt so at home with Mrs. Stedje. I could talk to her and tell her my heart. I think my interview with her enhanced my self-confidence, and it wasn't long before I went back to Mrs. Teal and told her that I wanted to do whatever it would take to be the first in my family to graduate with honors. Mrs. Teal arranged my schedule for the next year and told me that I would have to pass Algebra I by working for hours on my own in the summer. I assured her that I was ready to do just that!

One night I was visiting my brother, Marco, and his wife. I glanced in my little niece's toy box. There on top of all the other toys was an Smart Phone. *What?* I had purchased my phone at Wal-Mart, and it didn't work half of the time. I asked my brother, "What is that?"

He said, "Oh, it's an old one of mine, and I just gave it to our little girl to play with." I turned it on. It worked! My brother was still paying for the service for it. He threw it at me and asked me if I would like to buy it.

"You know I can't afford it." I retorted.

"As long as your grades are good, Noemy and I will pay for it," he said. So, I was to take them my report card every time. As long as I took care of my grades, the phone was mine to use.

As soon as school was out, I started coming to school Monday thru Friday all summer long. I worked in the computer lab by myself, teaching myself Algebra I. It was so hard, and sometimes, I would just get stuck. I would call Mrs. Teal at home, and she would walk me through my problem areas over the phone. Some days I just wanted to quit. Was it worth it?

I continued to work every day. I completed the first semester with a 78. Mrs. Teal was so proud of me. Her encouragement kept me going. The second semester, I made an even higher grade, finishing with a solid B in the class.

I started my junior year, and Mrs. Teal had warned me that this was going to be a most difficult year. I was taking both Math Models and Geometry. I told Mrs. Teal I was willing to drop football if I could not do my class work. Every night I spent my evenings doing mounds of homework, but I found myself determined to make it work. *I will do whatever it takes. I've got to do this!*

Saul's Junior Year

I worked hard so I would not have to quit football. I was on the starting lineup playing right tackle on offense. I loved the opportunity to slam my body into other players. It was then that I could put the world aside; It was a release for me. I still had a lot of pent-up emotions, and I had to find time for everything. My mind was filled with everything I needed to do. That year we had a good year--we were District Co-Champions. It felt so good to be on top for once in my life.

One night during Christmas vacation, my parents started arguing, and the argument just got worse and worse.

We had been through so much together. My dad was so my hero, and yet, there he was, making my mom cry. I wanted to fight him, yet he was my father, and I loved him. I left so I could think. I didn't want to be around him and be disrespectful to him. Yet, he was letting me down. I got so tired of listening to them and having to deal with it. I grabbed my coat and stepped outside. The cold was so bitter, but I was so hot I didn't even notice the freezing temperature. I started walking. I walked....and I walked....and I walked, the adrenalin coursing through my veins. I had walked fifteen miles to town, but by the time I got there, I was freezing. I had arrived at my brother's house. My brother said, "Saul, you know you have a room here." It was the first time I had walked out on my parents. I had to realize that my dad was human and made mistakes just like everyone else. I would just wait and see what happened. At the end of Christmas break, I went back to the house so I could be there for Mom.

Even though things were rough at home, Mrs. Teal could tell that I was a better, more dedicated student. One day Mr. Seagler, our principal, read the announcements. He said, "Those students with an overall GPA of 90 are eligible to apply for the National Honor Society." Mrs. Teal asked me if I had turned in my application. I said, "I'm not going to apply. If I wasn't good enough for them last year, then I don't want to be a part of it." She told me that I was silly and that I had earned that right to apply. "Besides," she said, "applying for the NHS is a reflection of all that you have accomplished." I relented and turned in my application.

I was needing fewer and fewer accommodations in the classroom. My three-year reevaluation showed that, according to test results, I no longer qualified to be in special education. I could now function in the classroom without that crutch! Mrs. Teal told me that I could ask her for help anytime-- that I didn't have to be in special education to do that. I felt like a baby eagle on the edge of a cliff. Would I soar or would I fall to the ground?

One morning I arrived at school. Korbin ran up to me and told me that he had been to my brother's house that morning to pick me up. I wasn't there. I was at my parents' house. "Saul, you've been accepted into NHS, and we were going to kidnap you this morning for the NHS breakfast." Mrs. Gillispie, the NHS sponsor, met me in the hall, handed me a letter and said, "Saul, congratulations, we are so proud of you! You are now a member of the Gruver High School NHS." I couldn't believe it. Who would have ever thought that I would be inducted into the National Honor Society? After all those years of special education, and now I was eligible for the most elite academic organization on campus. My parents were so excited because they knew how much I had struggled in the past.

Coming to school was an escape for me from all the drama at home. Mom and Dad were still arguing. Their fighting became so intense that I just couldn't stand it. I asked my brother if I could come live with him, and I moved out of my parents house. Mom left Dad shortly after that. How could our family be so split apart?

One day Mrs. Spivey, my third grade teacher, came to the high school. She saw me in the hall and said, "Saul, what is wrong?"

"Nothing," I said, trying to conceal my lie.

She looked at me eye to eye, "Saul, tell me."

I told her about my family. I could tell she hurt for me. Full of compassion, she said, "If I can do anything...call me. I'll help you--whatever you need."

Things were going really well at school, and I was happy there. I would catch myself smiling as I walked down the hall, and then I would ask myself, *"What are you smiling about?"* I was more comfortable hiding behind my mask of anger. For so many years, I had been in pain, walking with a limp, and in special ed. Now my family was divided. I did not want to be vulnerable and let people see the real me, so I just put up an invisible wall. It was much safer than being vulnerable. Even though I turned people away, I chose anger so I would be safe. I was an army of one. I so wanted to go into the military. All I could think about was army, army, army. But then I thought about my leg - I couldn't even begin to pass the physical with my leg in the shape it was in.

So, with my wall of anger, I didn't have to explain anything because no one wanted to be around me. Yes, anger was my coping mechanism; I didn't even consider that God loved me and wanted me to lean on Him.

EVEN A WOUNDED LION WANTS TO ROAR

"It is better to live one day as a lion, than a thousand days as a lamb."

— **Unknown**

CHAPTER 13

CHAPTER 13

Work has a lot of advantages. That summer, I worked on the farm for Bart Thoreson--he had used me some during Spring Break, and offered me a job for the summer. I did different jobs all summer, and the time I spent alone was good for me. I would do manual labor like processing cattle and digging out weeds with a shovel. For three weeks I cleaned sweet corn when it was so hot and humid. It was late when I got home from work, so I would just eat something and crawl into bed. There wasn't a lot of time to spend goofing around. I couldn't believe I was about to be a senior. Where had the time gone? I was so looking forward to my senior year in football--we were going to win it all. I had been lifting weights, so I was ready.

Alone, I found myself having flashbacks about my life. *Is this what I really want out of life? If I keep this mask on, I can just work and do my own thing.* For several days, the flashbacks would take me deeper each day. The flashbacks of all my life and all the vulnerable moments plagued me. I tried to shake them off, but they just kept following me around. I felt like I might explode. I would come home at night exhausted. I was so thankful that I could work. That was one thing my parents had given me--a strong work ethic.

My brother and his wife took another job, and that meant that they would have to move. He offered to take me with them, but I decided I wanted to stay in Gruver. I liked the thought of living alone, but sometimes the loneliness was more than I could stand. It was bad at night when I would come home from work--nothing but a dark house and no food prepared for me to eat.

With the money I earned that summer, I made a down payment a 1999 Ford Mustang dark green convertible from my brother-in-law. I named her Becky--she was "my little girl." I could tell her all my problems, and she didn't talk back! I had to do without a lot of things and sacrifice some of my "wants," but it was worth it to have my own car. I would put the top down and drive out of town. I would pull over and wait for the sunset, listening to good music.

One evening I thought, "This is not what I want," and I started crying and praying. I would question God, and then I would beg Him, "God, please give me the strength I need." I repeated this pattern often, and one evening in particular,

I just cried out to God, "I can't do this again." I asked God, "God, please forgive me, forgive me for all my sins. Forgive me for not trusting You. Give me strength to get through all of this. I know you will help me."

By the time I got home, it was dark. I felt like my eyes had been opened. Really opened. I could breathe easier--the air wasn't so thick anymore. For the first time, I had turned everything over to God, and I knew He was there for me. Since then, He has never left me. I knew He would always be there for me, no matter what.

I finally realized that I had been acting like a monster. What was I thinking? What would I have become? When animals are wounded, their first reaction is to attack, even if someone is trying to help them. Apparently, that was the way I was acting. After asking God for His forgiveness, I had a new lease on life. This wounded lion wanted to roar. A lion walks tall. He doesn't have to look over his shoulder. He doesn't live in fear. He walks proudly and unashamed. For the first time in my life, I felt clean and renewed. I felt like I had the strength to face each day. That strength was an inner force that I had never known before.

In time, Dad went to Mom's and asked her for her forgiveness for the way he had treated her. Eventually she went back home to him. I was still working on the ranch, and had decided I didn't need my dad. I was even willing to drop out of school so I could take care of my mom. We would be okay. My mom had never let me down. I was determined to be there for her now.

It wasn't long before my dad came to me and apologized for the way he had acted. He was ashamed for the way he had let his family down. I knew he was sorry for the things he had done, but it was really hard for me to let it all go. Things eventually did get better with my dad, but I chose to remain at my brother's house; I just couldn't bear to have to deal with it all over again.

My parents were willing for me to live alone, but it wasn't like they had deserted me or as if I were estranged from them. Occasionally, I would go visit them, and then at other times, they would go buy groceries and bring food to my house. He has continued to pay my utility bills. One baby step at a time, my relationship with my dad grew stronger and stronger.

When school started, I didn't know how I was going to make everything work. *How would I make the payments on my car since I was playing football and could not work? I know God will help me; I just don't know how He will do it.* My brother dropped out of school his senior year, and it was very important to him that I graduate from high school. He knew it would be hard for me to work after school, so he decided to take up my car payments during the school months.

When I was working for Bart, I worked with a man named Sam Sanchez. He told me that he had purchased a house in town and that he was going to remodel it. He asked me if I would be willing to help him after football practice and during the weekends. I was working a little for Howard and Charlen, but my money was gone, and I had no other significant source of income. The tires on my car were bad--I needed to do something, so I told him I would help him.

Dad continued to offer to help me. I assured him that I was fine, but he would always say, "Call me if you need me." From time to time, Dad would put some money on my bank card. He and I have come a long way. I know that our renewed relationship made it easier on mom. She had been through so much. Would I ever be able to repay her?

"If we climb high enough, we will reach a height from which tragedy ceases to look tragic."

– **Ivan D. Yalom,**
When Neitzche Wept

CHAPTER 14

CHAPTER 14

"SUUUUUU-----CHILLLLLLLLLLLLLLLLLLL! Hey, Suchil! Coach Brockman, our lineman coach, was screaming at the top of his lungs. "Get on the field!"

Oh my gosh—what had I missed? How long had he been hollering at me? I had been so deep in thought, I wasn't even paying attention to the game! Without even thinking, I strapped on my helmet and ran onto the field. I had no idea what was going on. The pain in my leg was so intense that I had trouble focusing on anything else. The cold air blowing out of the north was bitter. All of a sudden, reality hit me square in the face. I had to play! It was Homecoming. I had been on the sidelines, and now he was calling my name. He needed me.

In the second half, Victor scored two more touchdowns to make the final score,

Gruver over Shamrock, 40-7. Our defense capitalized

on two interceptions and a couple of fumble recoveries as we held Shamrock to 148 yards total offense. It was the perfect Homecoming game!

After the game, Mom and Dad came onto the field with the other parents. Dad shook my hand and mom hugged me as they offered their congratulations. It was a good night. I ran to the field house to shower and then go home. Everyone was slapping each other on the back—we were all so excited we had won our Homecoming game. And hey, I was a part of that game! I wasn't just dressed up in a uniform--I was part of the team!

The 2012 Senior Football Players with Coach Felderhoff

We ended the season as District Champs, and because we were district champions for District 1-1A, we earned a bye for Bi-District. We then ended our season by playing Sudan for Area, but we gained much more than we lost. As a group, we had bonded tighter than ever--we were a team, we were one! The locker room memories were never-to-be-forgotten ones, and personally, I had risen above my own physical difficulties. It was a year to remember.

One day after Homecoming, Scott Curry, pastor of the First Baptist Church, was visiting in the library. He came to congratulate us on our win and tell us what a good job we had done. He invited me to come to Bible Study at his church on Sunday morning. He said that he and Mrs. Curry taught the high school class, and I could be part of the group. I told him I would go. It wasn't that I had anything against church, it was just that my family didn't attend church regularly, so I was not in the habit of going every Sunday. Mrs. Gillispie told me that I could sit with her during the church service after Bible Study, so that's exactly what I did. She was down front close to the piano, so, despite my shyness, I marched to the front of the church and sat on the second pew, piano-side. People were kind to me and told me that they were glad I had come to church. Dr. Bob Adams came up to me after the service and told me that he was glad I was there. I had been in Boys Club with him several years earlier. Howard and Charlen were there, too, and they were glad to see me at church. The feeling that welled up inside me was one of peace and comfort. I liked being there, and I liked the sweet spirit that surrounded me. Every Sunday that I didn't have to work, I was determined to go back to church. For once in my life, I felt good about myself, and I appreciated everything that I had. Without a doubt, God was taking care of me.

Saul, Mrs. G and Cole

In February, we were to have our Junior/Senior Prom. I had already decided I wasn't going to go. I didn't have the money for a tuxedo, and besides it was just too much trouble.

On my birthday on January 17, I got an anonymous birthday card with $150.00 cash in it. The card said, "Use this to rent your tuxedo for the prom." *What? Who gave me this?*

There was a young lady who kept asking me who I was taking to the prom. Now that I had money for a tux, I really didn't have an excuse. So I made arrangements to go with her. We had a great time--it was a fun night. *Why were people being so nice to me?*

Saul speaking at Baptist Men's Breakfast

Dr. Adams caught me one Sunday after church and asked me if I would be willing to speak to the Baptist Men's Breakfast on a Saturday morning. "What do you want me to say?" I asked.

"I want you to just tell your story," he said. *Tell my story. What would they think?* On Saturday morning,

April 6, I went to the Men's Breakfast and stood and told them my story. To be able to stand and tell them how much God had done for me through all of the hardships in my life was a very healing moment for me. It made me even more grateful to God. To express it all verbally reminded me that God had a plan and a purpose for my life. I was glad I had said "yes" to His call.

Saul with a group of the men.

I continued to work hard at school. My Algebra II class was extremely difficult for me, but with help, I managed to make good grades. The pressure was on. As seniors, we would find out our class rank and overall GPA at the end of the fifth six weeks. I knew I was borderline, yet it was so important for me to graduate with honors. Graduating with honors would be the highest tribute I could pay to my parents for all of their sacrifices and hard work. They wanted nothing more than to see that I got a good education. For weeks my emotions went up and down. I struggled between highs and lows, worrying about my grades. Mrs. Gillispie just reminded me to do the very best that I could do, and then to just turn it over to God. I wanted to do that, but I so wanted to do this one thing for my mom. She deserved everything I could give her, and that included my very best.

*"Be strong when you are weak,
Brave when you are scared,
And humble when you are victorious."*

— **Unknown**

CHAPTER 15

CHAPTER 15

April 29, 2013. 10:30 A. M. The invitation said my parents were invited to the Academic Awards Program in the New Gym. *Did this mean I was getting a class award? Or did I receive the invitation because I was in NHS? Or could it possibly mean I was graduating with honors? No way!* My mom said she was coming to the program. I didn't want her to be disappointed.

At 10:15 on Monday morning, we were dismissed from class to go to the gym. The NHS organization all sat together on the floor. Mr. Seagler gave the welcome and then introduced Mrs. Gillispie as the NHS Adviser. She called my name and asked me to come forward. The NHS was presenting an award for the very first time--the "Above and Beyond Academic Award." She explained that this award was not to be given every year. It would be given only when a student should receive special recognition for academic achievement that was "above and beyond the call of duty." She told my story about being in special education and the effort I put into my school work to get out of special ed and be on a regular diploma plan. And then she said it--she said that I was graduating *with honors*! I couldn't believe my ears! For four years I had worked so hard to keep my grades an overall A average. There were days I thought I could never achieve that feat. There were days that I was tired of trying--I just wanted to quit and goof off with the rest of my friends.

Then there were days that I would think about my mom and dad and all of their sacrifices for me. And then I thought, *failure is not an option!* I thought about my mom giving up her home and household belongings to come to the United States. I thought about my dad being willing to work at menial jobs just so I could have a chance at a better education. I thought about my parents giving up their native language to come to a country where it was necessary for them to learn another language. I thought about them giving up their culture for a new way of life. They sacrificed it all so we could have a better education and a more prosperous life. Tears filled my eyes as I reflected on their lives and on all the things they had done for me.

Mr. Seagler then took the platform and began to call out the names of all the honor students. He started at the beginning of the alphabet. Of course, I would be toward the end!

And then it was my turn. "Saul Suchil." As I walked toward Mrs. Gillispie, I saw the smile on her face and the tears in her eyes as she raised her arms to put the honor cords around my neck. What a moment!

As I walked back to my chair, I glanced up in the audience. There sat Mom, smiling from ear to ear, wiping the tears that were cascading down her cheeks. The joy that shone through her tears radiated the love and devotion she had pledged to me so long ago.

Yes, Mom, we have come a long way. We did it. We did it together. I smiled through my own tears as I gave her a thumbs up!

*"Yesterday is history,
Tomorrow is a mystery,
But today is a gift.
What you do with it
is your choice."*

– Unknown

BETWEEN THE LORD AND ME

Lord,

How can I say thank You enough for not giving up on me and for loving me even when I doubted You? Thank You for protecting me and always being by my side. Thank You for bringing so many people into my life to teach me, to encourage me, and to walk with me in this life journey.

Thank You for my parents—what would I do without them? Thank You for the vision that You gave to them to bring their children to the United States so we could have a better education and lifestyle. Thank you for giving them the strength to carry on even when they did not feel like it.

Thank You for my brother, Marco, and my sister, Cindy. They have stood by me and supported and loved me all through my life.

Thank you for all the teachers and mentors in my life who encouraged me, taught me, and walked with me when life was so tough. Thank You for my school and for the "village" that raised me.

And now, yes, now, thank You for my trials—for my injuries—for my surgery—for all the hardships that molded me. They made me who I am—a stronger person who knows You and depends on You.

And You--the Lamb of God, the Lion of Judah--You were once a wounded lion, too, weren't You? Your wounds make my wounds seem so small. Thank You most of all for dying on the cross for my sins, so that I can be forgiven and spend eternity with You.

I love You,
Saul

Mrs. Stedje so eloquently expressed in just a few sentences, the story of my life:

"I believe Saul's life is a testimony of God's care and provision. Saul has faced many difficulties, but he has also been provided with ways to overcome them. His life has not been easy, but it is beautiful. I have absolutely no doubt that the challenges he has faced are great preparations for great accomplishments in the future."

"I regret nothing in my life even if my past was full of hurt, I still look back and smile, because it made me who I am today."

– **Unknown**

THIS IS NOT THE END...
IT IS ONLY THE BEGINNING!

www.ingramcontent.com/pod-product-compliance
Lightning Source LLC
Chambersburg PA
CBHW070448050426
42451CB00015B/3396